Cryptocurrency

Cryptocurrency basics step by step

volume 1

Kelly Fenathra

Copyright © 2019

All right reserved. No portion of this book may be reproduced, stored in a retrieval system, or transmitted in any form or by any means – electronic, mechanical, recording or otherwise – except for brief quotation in printed reviews without the prior written permission of the publisher or the author.

Copyright © 2019 Kelly Fenathra

TABLE OF CONTENT

Copyright © 2019 3

Introduction 7

1. History of Cryptocurrency 9
2. What is Cryptocurrency? 14
3. What are the benefits of cryptocurrency? 20
4. Benefits of cryptocurrencies 21
5. Scarcity supports value 21
6. It is fast 22
7. Privacy protection 22
8. No financial retribution 23
9. Cheaper transfers 23
10. Fewer barriers to international transactions
    24
11. No third parties 24
12. What is Mining? 25
13. Cryptocurrency Purchases 30
    1. Bitfinex 33

2. Robinhood 33
3. OKEx 34
4. Binance 34
5. Bitmex 34
Conclusion 36

Introduction

Technology has transformed the financial world. Today there are multiple platforms, payment options and products that make monetary transactions easier for people all over the world. One of such technological breakthroughs in the financial sector is cryptocurrency. What we now know as digital money started years ago with very little relevance. Today, it has grown in leaps and bounds enough to get the attention of investors.

This book is a step by step guide of how cryptocurrency works. If you have heard about crypto coins in the past, you are about to dive even deeper from a beginner's perspective. There are a lot of speculations on the modus operandi of crypto coins; people are wondering how it works, is it sustainable? Can anyone invest? What about the risks involved? These questions make cryptocurrency seem like a very complex idea.

Although there are some technical terms, you must get acquainted with, but if you are focused on the process by paying attention to every detail, you will be able to grasp the essential aspects and excel as a crypto investor, buyer or seller. In the chapters below, you will be exposed to detailed ides about crypto coins, the concept of mining, blockchain technology and even tips on trading.

It is expected that when you get to the end of this book, you will be equipped with the right set of information and tools that will help you make the right decisions when investing. Despite the crypto market being volatile, you can still make huge investments and get amazing rewards.

You must realize that the cryptocurrency journey is a never-ending one; what we knew about cryptos five years ago is entirely different from what is obtainable right now. The continuous search for updated information will make it easier for you to stay ahead with this technological breakthrough.

We have had enough with the first talks; it is time to get started. The first chapter takes you back to the history of cryptocurrency; for you to understand the present and future, you must have a glimpse into the past. Flip over to the next chapter and get started now.

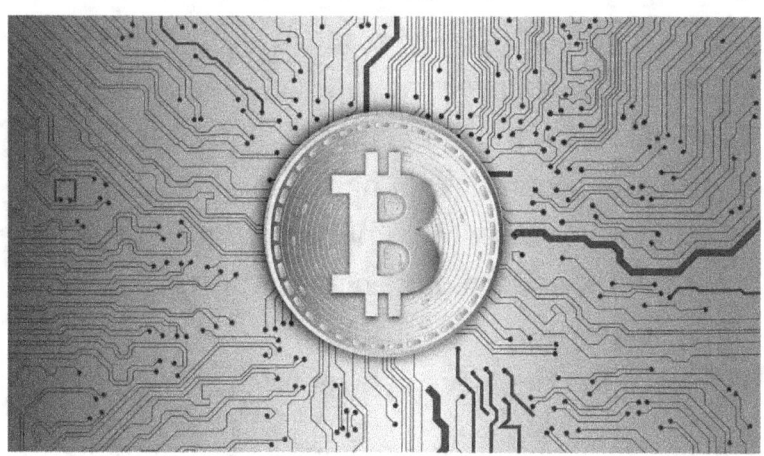

1. History of Cryptocurrency

Cryptocurrencies existed as a theoretical construct before the first digital currencies became known. The earliest proponents of cryptocurrencies shared the idea that the application of cutting-edge mathematical and computer science principles will solve the shortcomings of fiat currencies.

Traditional currencies pose some severe challenges that make transactions difficult for users especially those who seek to carry out international transfers beyond borders. The technical foundations of cryptos date back to the early 1980s when David Chaum an American cryptographer invented a blinding algorithm which is central to modern day encryption. The algorithm made secure and unalterable information exchange to take place between parties.

The works of David Chaum laid the groundwork for the future of electronic currency transfers popularly known as blinded money. By late 1980's David Chaum also enlisted the help of some cryptocurrency devotees to commercialize the idea behind blinded money. When he got to the Netherlands, he created DigiCash, a profit company that crafted units of currency based on the algorithm.

Now unlike the Bitcoin and other cryptocurrencies that sprang forth, later, DigiCash's wasn't decentralised because Chaum's organisation had the monopoly on supply control (this is quite similar to the central bank's monopoly on fiat currencies).

DigiCash dealt with individuals directly at first, but the Netherland authorities didn't like it, so they had to sell to licensed banks. Microsoft wanted a partnership with DigiCash, and due to a disagreement on terms, the companies couldn't conclude.

As DigiCash went belly-up, Chaum's associate developed and released a cryptocurrency known as BitGold. BitGold used blockchain technology but never gained widespread recognition as such it was not a viable means of exchange or payment. Just after DigiCash a lot of research and investment was done to discover ideas around electronic financial transactions.

A lot of mobile payment intermediaries sprang up of which PayPal was a significant lead. E-gold became a favorite digital gold buying organization

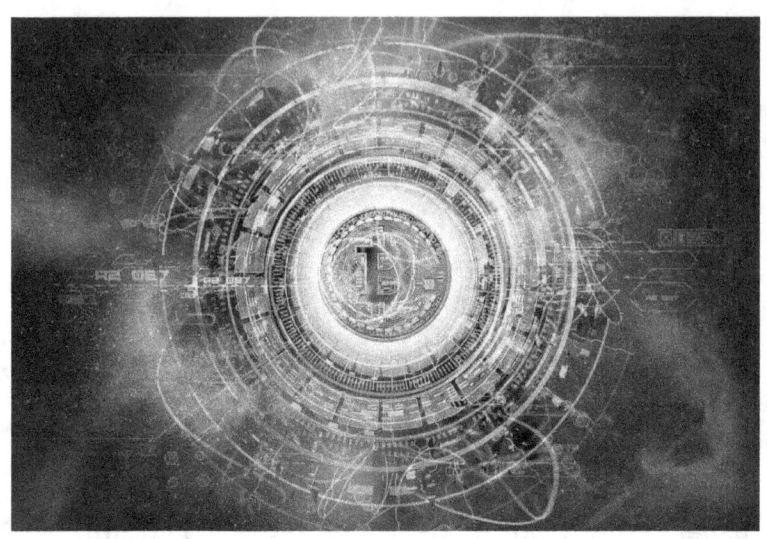

as well. E-gold didn't last for a very long time, and then it paved the way for Bitcoin which is known as the first modern cryptocurrency.

The Bitcoin was the first means of exchange that combined decentralized control, the anonymity of users and record-keeping blockchain. Bitcoin was first outlined in 2008 on a white paper that was published by Satoshi Nakamoto. In 2009, Bitcoin was released, and some individuals started to exchange and my currencies, by 2010, other crypto coins emerged.

By 2012, some organizations such as WordPress started to accept payment in Bitcoin. This paved the way for the acceptance of Bitcoin while helping the crypto build firm competition against fiat currencies. The more people utilized the Bitcoin, the more popular it became, and this gave investors and financial technology enthusiasts an insight into how successful cryptocurrencies will be.

Bitcoin created a world of possibilities for other crypto coins, and since then it has been the leading cryptocurrency world over. The history of cryptocurrency is one laced with the determination to unravel solutions that make the process of payment and financial transactions seamless. The problems banks and societies experience with fiat currencies no longer hold sway for those who seek answers with cryptocurrencies.

This chapter has been all about the history of cryptocurrency and how this digital currency platform became very prominent in the world today. The future of cryptocurrencies cannot be understood without an appreciation of the past first. Everything you have learnt in this chapter will help shape the cryptocurrency narrative you encounter in the next sections.

Now that we know how cryptocurrency came about, it is time to discover what the term means. The next chapter elucidates on the concept of cryptocurrency in particular; what it means and how you can take advantage of it in this 21st century.

2. What is Cryptocurrency?

Cryptocurrency refers to digital money; this is a type of currency that can be used to carry out transactions between individuals regardless of their location. Cryptocurrencies also referred to as virtual currencies were created by private individuals or groups, and they are not regulated by national governments. Cryptocurrencies are considered an alternative means of financial exchange that exist beyond the boundaries of monetary policy.

With cryptocurrencies, cryptographic protocols and complex codes are used to encrypt sensitive data transfers. Cryptocurrency developers build protocols on advanced mathematics and engineering making it difficult for the system to be duplicated or hacked into. The protocols also protect the identities of crypto users thus making transactions and fund transfer challenging to trace to specific groups.

Cryptocurrencies work with a decentralized control; this means that the supply and value systems are controlled by the activities of users and complex protocols built with codes. No central regulatory authorities are monitoring the process. Miners can also leverage on the computing power to record transactions while creating new cryptos paid by other users.

Additionally, cryptocurrencies can be exchanged for fiat currencies online. Every coin has a variable exchange rate with the currencies in the world such as Dollars, British Pound, European Euro etc. You should know that cryptocurrencies are vulnerable to hacks and thefts perpetrated by cybercriminals.

However, there is a finite supply of cryptocurrencies. There are specific instructions on the source codes that outline the exact number of units that will ever exist. It has become increasingly difficult for miners to produce crypto units and when the limit is reached new cryptos will no longer be produced.

One feature of cryptocurrency is the fact that transactions can be done speedily across borders. With fiat currencies, there are no immediate assurances of recipients getting funds, especially concerning international payments. These particular challenges with fiat are taken care of with crypto coins as it offers a safer, faster and more reliable way of transacting funds. There is also the elimination of third parties with transactions as the numerous paperwork and bankers needed to make transfers possible with fiat aren't required with cryptocurrencies.

Cryptocurrencies work effectively through the source codes and technical controls that support its systems. When you think about the effectiveness of cryptocurrencies and why it works, you should remember the four primary features that make it work, they are;

1. **Security**
2. **Reliability**
3. **Anonymity**
4. **Values**

There are several types of crypto coins available currently in the market. The Bitcoin created an avenue for these coins to thrive as such other types of coins has made the market much more flexible. Users now have a pool of coins to choose from before making investment decisions.

Before you decide to invest with any coin, you will have first to carry out research first and ensure that you are making the right decision.

The cryptocurrency market is a very volatile one that demands a lot of caution; I always advise that you start investing, trading or buying with tiny sums of money. Starting small will help you study the market, learn and make progress as you trade.

We have considered the history of cryptocurrency and discovered the basics of digital currencies. The next chapter takes us to the next level of our journey as we discuss the advantages and benefits of cryptocurrencies. If you get involved with this process, you've got to know what is in store for you and the kind of progress you will make with

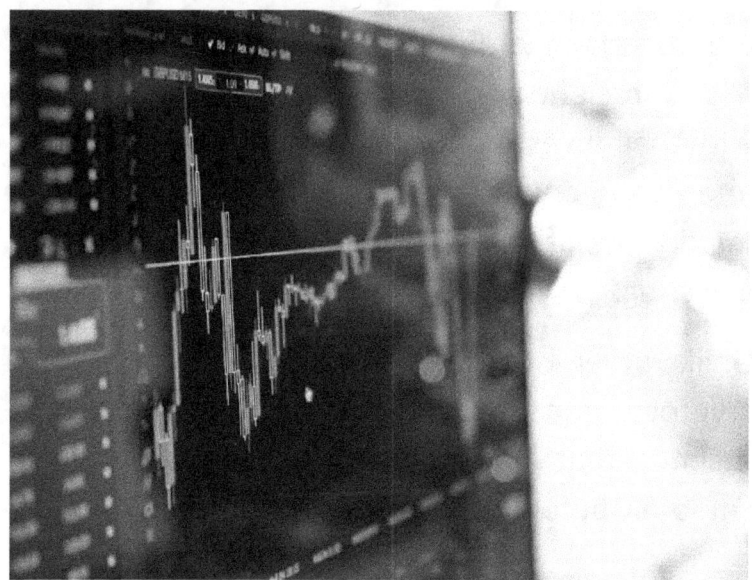

investments.

3. What are the benefits of cryptocurrency?

Cryptocurrencies are quite volatile, but they have a lot of benefits for investors who can be smart with their investments. Before we get to the interests of cryptos, you should understand the importance of being careful with money before investing.

Unlike other investment options, if you lose cryptocurrencies, you lose them for them. So, it is essential that you use the money you can let go of smoothly before making the investments.

Always utilize money that wouldn't cause a strain on you financially should anything go wrong. By being mindful with your crypto investments will help you make the right decisions with the right coins.

So, what are the benefits of cryptocurrencies?

4. Benefits of cryptocurrencies

5. Scarcity supports value

Most cryptocurrencies are crafted for deficiency; this is a feature that shows the extent of units that will ever exist.

Crypto coins are very valuable tenders, and recently, they have proven to compete in terms of value with fiat. They do offer inflation protection which is unavailable to fiat currency users.

6. It is fast

Cryptocurrency transactions are speedy. The average crypto transfer that is done on an international level is faster than a domestic transfer done on the same level. When you transfer funds to someone else, you will see the transaction get confirmed, and the recipient receives it within minutes.

7. Privacy protection

There are two significant features of cryptocurrencies that make it very attractive for users; these are privacy and anonymity. Cryptocurrency users can employ the use of pseudonyms that are not connected to their personal information or accounts of users. There are layers of protections made possible by the crypto-security which ensures that personal details are not utilized nor compromised.

8. No financial retribution

In some countries, it is always easy for those in authorities to freeze the assets and private bank accounts of very wealthy individuals especially those who are in violation of the ruling party's decisions.

Cryptocurrencies are immune from authoritarian caprices, the funds and records for cryptos are stored in various locations around the world. So, this means that it will be impossible for the government to take over the assets or investment of crypto users.

9. Cheaper transfers

The security of cryptocurrency makes it easier for payment to be authenticated thus eliminating the need for other payments processes that attract extra charges. Cryptocurrency charges are usually less than 1% of the transaction value, and this competes successfully against the 1.5% to 3% paid for credit card processors and PayPal.

10. Fewer barriers to international transactions

International transactions are not handled differently from domestic ones. Deals with cryptos are free or come with a nominal fee regardless of where the senders and recipients are located. Users of fiat currencies always must pay some special fees for international transactions, and at the end of the day, such transfers can be delayed.

11. No third parties

With cryptocurrencies, there are no third parties! You get to transact with the recipient of your funds directly thus eliminating the stressful processes that are caused by third parties in banking institutions. This feature of the absence of third parties makes it possible for investors and users of crypto coins to trust the process even more and experience seamless transactions.

The benefits of cryptocurrencies make it a desirable investment option. With cryptocurrencies, you can get the best out of the most exciting investment offer that is taking over the world. There are specific cryptocurrency processes you must get used to, and one of them is Mining; in the next chapter, you will read every aspect of mining and how it contributes to making cryptocurrency easy to use.

12. What is Mining?

Mining is a process through which transactions for various cryptocurrencies are verified and added to the blockchain digital ledger. Mining is also known as crypto coin mining; altcoin mining or Bitcoin mining and it has raised interest as a topic and activity thus increasing the growth of crypto coins.

Every time a cryptocurrency transaction is done, there is a miner responsible for ensuring the authenticity of the information. When the details are verified the blockchain is updated with transaction details. The mining process entails a stiff competition between miners to solve complicated mathematical problems using a cryptographic hash function that is associated with a block containing the transaction data.

When a cryptocurrency miner cracks a code, he is rewarded. The reward is the privilege to authorize the transaction, and in return, the miner earns a small amount of cryptocurrency for himself. To maintain the competition with other miners the miner needs to have specialized hardware.

You can become a miner if you are interested in the process and want to earn some more cryptos. However, you should know that cryptocurrencies

rise in popularity and value as such competition

increases. This means that organizations with more extensive resources and tools that most individuals cannot afford.

For you to start mining, you will need computer hardware that has a specialized graphics processing unit chip or an application-specific integrated circuit (ASIC). There is also a need for enough cooling means for the device, steady internet connection, a cryptocurrency mining software package and the membership of an online cryptocurrency exchange as well as an online mining pool.

Miners are record-keepers for cryptocurrency communities, and they use highly technical methods to verify the completeness, security and accuracy of currencies block chains. Miners create with new cryptocurrency units, and they can get up to 1% of the transaction value that is paid by buyers.

Though mining produces new cryptos most of the cryptocurrencies are designed to have a finite supply (which is a guarantee of value). This means that miners get fewer new units per new blockchain. The last Bitcoin unit will be mined in the 22nd century, so this gives miners enough time to get the most out of the mining experience for now.

Mining presents an opportunity for individuals and organizations to enjoy some benefits of being a part of the cryptocurrency process. With mining, you also gain insight into the coins that are

trending and the best choices to make when investing. Miners always have first-hand information on the coins people can utilize and the coins that are vulnerable; this is a useful feature that makes mining a beautiful aspect of cryptocurrency.

How can cryptocurrencies be purchased? Get answers and more to the questions asked above in the next chapter as we explore cryptocurrency purchases.

13. Cryptocurrency Purchases

When you make up your mind to get involved with cryptocurrencies, the first step you must take is to buy the coins. As it is with every other investment, you must first have access to the tender and then use them to achieve success with your finances. So, in this chapter, you will learn some of the best ways through which crypto coins can be purchased.

The most common place to buy crypto coins and trade with them is on an exchange. Exchanges are the places where you buy and sell crypto using fiat currencies, and there are various ways to ascertain how reliable the transaction is as well as its liquidity, spread fees, purchase and withdrawal limits, security, insurance, trading volume and user-friendliness. One of the very best exchanges you can use is Coinbase; it has a very user-friendly interface you can rely on when making a purchase.

For you to transfer crypto coins from exchanges to your hardware wallet for long-term storage, all you must do is follow through with these straightforward steps.

1. **Plug your KeepKey USB Cable**

2. **Open the KeepKey client on Google Chrome**

3. **Find your wallet address on the KeepKey Client UI**

4. **Gain access to Coinbase and click on the "Send/Request" tab.**

5. **Input your KeepKey wallet address**

6. Confirm the amount and click on "Send Funds."

Make sure that you send only little amounts to test if the purchase process works before posting in bulk. If an error occurs in the process and you send huge sums, you might lose your coins and never regain them. There might be a small transfer fee charged at this point.

Some banks no longer allow users to utilize their credit card for crypto purchases, but there are still available options through which you can buy coins. If you are going to use Coinbase, you must first create an account and verify your identity then buy coins using your debit card.

Coinbase also has another company known as GDAX; a platform that gives users another idea of how crypto exchanges work. The platform has an intuitive interface with charting tools and trade history. These are the tools you will need as a trader to make sure you get the best out of your trade.

There are other exchanges you can utilize as a trader to purchase coins, some of these exchanges are mentioned below;

1. Bitfinex

This is a viral exchange that became popular in 2012; the website has been considered as the most advanced cryptocurrency trading platform currently. With an app that can be used by Android and iPhone, this exchange boost of three key features; exchange training, margin funding and margin trading.

2. Robinhood

This is quite a unique exchange that has a zero-fee feature and a very easy to use the platform. You can buy Bitcoin and Ethereum from your phone with no trading fees.

3. OKEx

OKEx is very popular because it supports more than 145 cryptocurrencies. The platform has its cryptocurrency known as OKB, and it has experienced over $1.5 million in bitcoin future daily. This is one of the most trusted global cryptocurrency exchanges in the world.

4. Binance

Being one of the world biggest cryptocurrency exchange comprising wallet, labs, charity info etc. Binance has got its coin referred to as BNB, and it comes at a discount when there is a crypto-to-crypto payment.

5. Bitmex

This exchange is a premier Bitcoin exchange that is based in Hong Kong; it is also the largest cryptocurrency according to market capitalization. According to reports, Bitmex has done over 2 billion USD transactions within 24 hours. The fact that it is an exchange that is easy to use makes it quite attractive for users and investors.

Purchasing cryptocurrencies is a step that makes you a full investor in crypto coins. You must have lessons from consistent trading that will aid your experience on this journey. While you trade huge amounts on trusted exchanges, test the other exchanges with little quantities until you are sure of their security and integrity.

Is there a connection between employment and cryptocurrencies? If there are, you will find the answers in the next section of this book; head over there now and enjoy the read.

Conclusion

Thank you for being such a great sport by reading through to the end. We are finally at the last section and I believe you have learnt a lot from the preceding chapters. Cryptocurrency continues to evolve with time, what you have read now is a beginner's guide, but you cannot afford to bring your quest for knowledge to an end.

You need to ask yourself "What's next?" at this point. How are you going to bring the words you've just read to life through action?

There are a whole lot of books, materials online and offline on how people can utilize cryptocurrencies. One can only wonder why people aren't making the right decisions with crypto coins.

I want you to know that it isn't enough to have access to information to know what to do with your cryptos. You need to become PROACTIVE with what you know now because it will determine what you achieve in the future. Now you know a lot about cryptocurrency, it is time to go out there and buy your first coins, invest, sell, watch the market closely while learning one step at a time.

You will not become a great investor because what you know, you will only become a very inspiring investor based on what you do with what you know.

Kick out the fear of making mistakes and be audacious; great investors don't fear failure, they make the most out of it. If you aren't doing something about what you know, then you aren't prepared for success.

This book is volume 1 in our series of cryptocurrency revelations. There will be other volumes, but the knowledge gained in this book serves as a foundation on which other volumes will be built upon.

There is so much for you to accomplish with what you know now; take definitive steps towards growing your investment portfolio by getting the best out of cryptocurrencies.

One of the most interesting and effective ways of getting the best out of this book is by sharing its content with others.

Knowledge shared is more knowledge gained.

When you share with others, you tend to discover more about what you share and build a community of crypto investors that make significant investment decisions. What are you waiting for? Set up that crypto club in your neighborhood, send this book as a gift to friends and family, consistently read and act together.

The world of digital currencies is going to be even more technical and developed as the years go by. There will be more opportunities to use cryptos, and that means investors will cash out of the surge. Monitor your progress every day and don't relent in your efforts to get better with your investments.

With cryptocurrency its WORK, WORK and more WORK!

Cheers to a fantastic crypto experience!

www.ingramcontent.com/pod-product-compliance
Lightning Source LLC
Chambersburg PA
CBHW071156220526
45468CB00003B/1054